DECEMBER 25, 1994

D0977421

Conversations
with My Cat

Also by David Fisher

Gracie,
with George Burns

The Naked Truth,
with Leslie Nielsen

The Umpire Strikes Back,
with Ron Luciano

*What's What: A Visual Glossary of
the Physical World,*
with Reg Bragonier

The War Magician

Killer, with "Joey"

The Pack

CONVERSATIONS
WITH MY CAT

David Fisher

VIKING

VIKING
Published by the Penguin Group
Penguin Books USA Inc., 375 Hudson Street,
New York, New York 10014, U.S.A.
Penguin Books Ltd, 27 Wrights Lane, London W8 5TZ, England
Penguin Books Australia Ltd, Ringwood, Victoria, Australia
Penguin Books Canada Ltd, 10 Alcorn Avenue,
Toronto, Ontario, Canada M4V 3B2
Penguin Books (N.Z.) Ltd, 182–190 Wairau Road,
Auckland 10, New Zealand

Penguin Books Ltd, Registered Offices:
Harmondsworth, Middlesex, England

First published in 1994 by Viking Penguin,
a division of Penguin Books USA Inc.

1 3 5 7 9 10 8 6 4 2

LIBRARY OF CONGRESS CATALOGING IN PUBLICATION DATA
Fisher, David.
Conversations with my cat/David Fisher.
p.   cm.
ISBN 0-670-85720-3
1. Cats—Humor. I. Title.
PN6231.C23F55 1994
818´.5402—dc20   94-20641

Printed in the United States of America
Set in Old Style 7
Designed by Kathryn Parise
Illustrations by Paul Yalowitz

To Dr. William "Skip" Sullivan,
DVM, Martha McDonnell, and Suzanne Terho
of The Cat Practice in New York City,
who so lovingly care for all of
The Bomber's friends.

The author would like to gratefully acknowledge the efforts of Patty Brown of John Boswell Associates to bring this book to life, Courtney Chandell for her continued support, and Mindy Werner of Viking, who laughed in all the right places.

CONVERSATIONS
WITH MY CAT

"**M**eow . . ." pleaded The Bomber, moving swiftly across the room to my side, rubbing against my leg in a manner sensuous yet submissive.

"Not now," I replied forcefully.

"Meooowww . . ." he repeated, a mournful cry rising from the depths of his hunger.

I looked at him and spoke slowly and distinctly. "I said, I will feed you in a little while." I struggled with the knot of my tie, a knot that signaled my acceptance of all the rules of civilized behavior.

With a desperation not of human origin, he whined once more, "Neooowww . . ."

I paused, my hands at my neck, and commanded him still with a look. He waited. "Don't you understand English?" I asked. "I said, not now."

"And I said, *nowww*," The Bomber said, and at

that instant the comfort of my world as I had known it ended forever.

A chill swept through my body. "Excuse me?" I asked politely, then waited for the silence I felt confident would follow. For the first time that night, I gave him my full attention.

Staring at me, his unblinking eyes black slits against an emerald field, he repeated, "I said, feed me now."

I found myself sitting down, though I have no memory of moving. He was sitting opposite me, curled gracefully in the seat of his favorite chair. "You can speak," I said, more a statement of wonder than a question.

"Several languages," he replied casually. "Tail, Plant, several dialects of Bird. I understand some Rodent, but I don't really speak it. Even a passable Rabbit, although I really have a hard time with their accent."

In an instant a million thoughts flashed through my mind. They seemed to have no beginning and no end, just the purity of knowledge. "I just . . ." I shook my head in bewilderment. "I never . . . I just never suspected you were so smart."

His ears were standing at alert, and he twisted their cups in my direction. "Why do you think I'm so smart? Just because I can speak English?"

"Well, yeah," I said with a nervous chuckle.

"So what does that say about all the Greeks?" he

< 2 >

asked. Then he glanced at Catfish, who was sitting on the arm of the couch, her head resting on her extended legs. Catfish was looking at him with reproachful eyes. Something passed between them, but I couldn't understand it. The Bomber looked back at me. "You think you're so smart, but you only speak English. I mean, you barely understand a wag of Tail. Dogs," he said disdainfully. "Even dogs understand Tail. You wouldn't know what to say with a tail if you had one."

Stunned, shocked, astonished did not begin to describe my condition. I had always known my cats were special, but even I had never dared imagine this. Politely, I would listen as others told me tales of their wondrous cats, and I would smile and nod at the appropriate points, but in my heart I knew the truth: Anything their cats could do, my cats could do cuter.

My cats, as I'd thought of them till this night, my cats: The Bomber, as bluish-gray as the mist of a London dusk, whose abundance lolled beneath him as he moved like a gentle tide flowing up a beach, and the smaller black female with a white apron and white boots I'd named Catfish. My cats, who knew me and understood me on a level spoken language could never approach. They had always been there for me when I needed their warmth, and in return I'd given them food and shelter and love. I had thought of them as my family, my children, and assumed that they thought of me simply as God.

Thought of me? Was it really possible? Like every cat owner, there were so many questions I'd long wondered about: Can my cats think? Do they have memories? Can they form ideas? Do they like me? I mean really, really like me? And if their personalities were embodied in human form, would I like them?

But I'd never expected to have my questions answered.

I was only beginning to appreciate the immensity of what was taking place in my living room: I was having a conversation with my cat. With a few words The Bomber had changed forever the relationship between man and animal. A new world had been opened to me. I realized the implications and, admittedly, the possibilities. This was the story of a lifetime, and my reportorial instincts took over. "Bomber," I asked, "would you mind . . . I mean, you mind if I turn on a tape recorder?"

Once again he looked at Catfish, who turned away. Was she disgusted with this display? The Bomber looked at me thoughtfully. His answer surprised me, though in fact it probably shouldn't have. It was the only answer he was capable of giving. When he spoke, he spoke with five thousand years of breeding. He asked, "What's in it for me?"

What's in it for me? After everything I'd done for him? I'd given him a good home, shelter on cold nights, a relatively clean litter box; I'd fed him and protected him from big dogs. "Well," I finally replied, in a voice so soft the words seemed too light to cut through the air, "what would you like?" Having never negotiated with a cat, I didn't know what to offer. Fish?

"For one thing, more respect," he said coldly. I studied his voice as he spoke; it was more resonant than I would have imagined, out of proportion to his size. He spoke clearly, although he had a labial *l*, rolling them gently into *r*s; I wondered if that was caused by his blunted nose, or if perhaps he'd learned to speak by listening to Tom Brokaw. Its pitch was somewhere between car and voice mail, the kind of pleasant, gender-neutral voice that insists your passenger-side door is open but would be glad to take a message. And he spoke with confidence, making it obvious he'd been preparing for this night. "Everything is always you, you, you," he continued. "Your needs, your problems, your desires. I'm sleeping peacefully on the chair and you decide you want to sit there"—his tail slashed angrily through the air for emphasis—"so you just push me away. You've never tried to understand my needs, my wishes. Me and . . ." With a tilt of his head, he indicated Catfish. She didn't move, although she lazily brushed her tail in acknowledgment. "We're always expected to respond to you. Has it ever occurred to you that sometimes I might be depressed?"

Although I was looking right at him, it was the

truth of his words I was seeing. He was absolutely right, of course. I had never considered his feelings when making decisions that affected all of us. We did what I wanted to do, when I wanted to do it. But what, I wondered, what did he have to be depressed about?

Before I could put that question to him, I knew with certainty that he had heard my thoughts. I'd always believed there was a communication between us that transcended spoken language—he knew when I was going to feed him long before I went into the kitchen; I knew when he felt his litter box was too dirty for him to use—but this revelation might have been the most shocking of all. The Bomber could read my thoughts!

"What did I have to be depressed about?" he asked aloud, interrupting my reverie. "Oh, I wonder?" I detected an edge of sarcasm in his voice. "Could it possibly be that only four days after I moved in here you took me to some butcher and paid him to cut off my manhood?"

My jaw dropped. "But . . . but they told me you had to be fixed," I protested.

"I wasn't broken," he hissed. "And let's see, what else might make me feel bad? How would you like it if you got to eat only twice a day, when somebody else decided to feed you? And if sometimes that somebody was too lazy to clean out one little dish before putting food in it. And . . ."

Oh, maybe once or twice, I thought, but . . .

. . . A week! he insisted. His thoughts were in my mind, too.

"And that stuff you feed us? I mean, have you ever stopped to consider exactly what's in meat by-products?"

Eight years had passed without him saying a single word, but like a burst dam the words now poured out of him.

He sat silent. "Okay," he said reluctantly, "go ahead. Put on your recorder."

Catfish stood and arched her back, a cat's yawn, then walked out of the room.

It took me only minutes to set up the machine. I laid the microphone in front of him and pressed the record button. "It's running," I said.

And with that, The Bomber began telling me the remarkable story of his life.

"I never knew my father," he started, then paused. I thought I detected a sadness in his voice as he added, "I don't even know my own birthday."

Until this night I'd thought I knew everything there was to know about The Bomber, his habits, his likes and dislikes—loves country music, hates Nine Lives Mocha Fish—but as he spoke, it became clear how little I had ever known about who he really was beneath his soft fur and cold, wet nose.

"I was born in a cardboard box, without a roof over my head," he continued. "There were five of us, three boys, two girls. Life was tough, but somehow my mother managed to keep us together. Maybe we didn't have much, but thanks to her we always knew where our next meal was coming from. More than 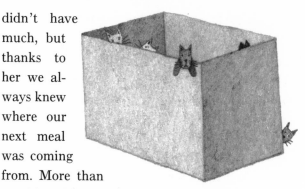 anything else, though, my mother instilled in all of us a great sense of pride in who we were.

"She was a teacher, and right from the beginning she taught us how to survive. She had a little saying for everything. 'You can never have too many mice,' she used to say, or, 'A mouse in the paw is worth two in the insulation.' And it was from my mother that we learned how to deal with people. There are good people and there are bad people, she taught us, but in the end they are all people. When it came right down to it, we had to depend on ourselves. 'There's a good reason cats say *me*-ow,' she pointed out, 'rather than *you*-ow or *we*-ow.'

"Practically the very first thing she taught us, when we were just tiny little kits, was the single most important rule that any cat ever learns, the golden rule of cats that governs all relationships we have with people: You scratch my back, you scratch my back."

I was so engrossed in his story that the first ring of

< 8 >

the telephone sent a shock through my system. The insistent tone seemed to come from another world. The Bomber paused. "It's not for me," he said.

It was Alice. "Where are you?" she asked in a very controlled voice. "You were supposed to be here an hour ago. Our reservation . . ."

"I'm really sorry," I blurted out, then said as calmly as possible, "I want you to listen to me very carefully. Now, you're probably not going to believe this . . ."

"Coming from you? Oh, I believe that."

". . . but I've been sitting here having an intelligent conversation with The Bomber."

"It's another basketball game, isn't it, David?" she asked, completely ignoring my statement. "Just tell me the truth."

"I *am* telling you the truth," I insisted. "I know it sounds crazy, but just as I was getting ready to leave, The Bomber started speaking to me. And you wouldn't expect me to just walk out, would you? I mean, my cat is talking!"

After a long pause, she said without emotion, "David, I don't know what to do anymore. I know you love your cats, but don't you think . . . don't you think that your relationship with them is sort of unhealthy?"

"You're right, I was watching a basketball game." It was obvious she would never believe me. Truthfully, I wasn't sure I believed it myself. A cat speaking? It didn't seem possible. But I was caught in a terrible dilemma: I had to choose between continuing to speak to my cat and never again speaking to my girlfriend.

Alice won. I promised to meet her at the restaurant as soon as possible. The Bomber was scratching behind his ear with his rear paw, a look of ecstasy on his face. For an instant, I wondered if I had imagined the whole thing. A cat speaking? "That was Alice," I said, clearing my throat. Alice, the woman I'd been dating for more than a year, had formed her own distant but respectful relationship with both The Bomber and Catfish. She was friendly enough, although she treated them like animals. I'd always assumed they liked her, too, but suddenly I wasn't so sure. "So," I asked casually, "what do you really think about her?"

The Bomber swished the very end of his tail slowly from side to side; somehow I understood that this was a cat shrug. "She's all right, I guess," he said. "Personally, I don't know how anybody could be interested in a female who's got only two breasts."

I smiled. It was nice to know that my cat had a sense of humor. I turned off the tape recorder and got ready to leave. As I walked toward the door I absentmindedly leaned over to scratch his head, just as I'd done almost every time I'd left the apartment in the eight years we'd been together. But

< 10 >

this time I hesitated, my hand suspended in midair.

He glanced up at it. "Sure," he said in a friendly tone, "go ahead." I scratched his head for old times' sake, but both of us realized that our relationship would never be the same again.

As I closed the door, I shouted to him, "See you later."

"Don't make too much noise when you come in," he replied, then added, "And would you pick up some Evian on your way back. That tap water has a funny taste."

I desperately needed to confide in someone. At the magazine the next day, I walked into the office of the articles editor, Lorraine LeTac, remembering that she kept framed pictures of two sort of ugly cats on her desk. "I know this sounds silly, Lorraine," I said, "but do your cats ever speak to you?"

"You mean, like, do they make sounds to express their needs?"

"No, I mean do they tell you what they want in English?"

She pursed her lips as she thought about it. "Well, they don't exactly speak," she said. Then she added enthusiastically, "But they do math, if that helps."

"What do you mean?"

"Well, like, I'll say to Buck, 'If I buy eight cans of cat food and feed you two cans a day for four days, how many cans will I have left?'"

"And what does he say?"

"Nothing. I mean, he's really a very smart cat." Then she smiled broadly.

I left the office early that day. I'd planned to have dinner with an attorney because I was interested in doing a piece about one of his mob cases, but I canceled, pleading a headache. That was the first appointment I changed to spend the evening with The Bomber. It would not be the last.

The Bomber was asleep in my chair, luxuriating in the warmth of my lamp, when I opened the door. "I'm home," I announced with false cheer. I don't know what I expected to hear in response. Maybe some part of me was worried it might be silence.

He lifted his head an inch. "You're early," he noted, and yawned.

The initial shock had worn off, replaced by incredible excitement. In my rent-stabilized apartment, in the middle of New York City, the world of human beings and the world of animals were speaking to each other for the first time. A dream . . . More than a dream, a fantasy come true: the ultimate barrier between the species had been surmounted. There were so many things I wanted to know that even before he'd finished answering one question I was asking two more.

That second night we discussed the differences between man and . . . not man. Once again, we were sitting in the living room with my tape recorder be-

< 12 >

tween us, though this time I let Bomber remain in my chair. Catfish was in the bedroom watching television. I sensed a tension between the two of them that I'd never noticed, and it was something I meant to explore. Eventually.

As Bomber licked the last of his sushi off his plate, he pointed out that one of the real difficulties in communicating with another species was language. "See, when *you* give a person a licking, it's considered a bad thing," he explained, "but when I give a person a licking, it's considered a gesture of affection."

Then he began comparing people and cats. "People think; cats feel. You think before you act." He paused, then added, "Well, at least you're supposed to. But we feel, then we act. You think about your feelings; we just feel. The Urge, we call it; sometimes the Big Urge. It's really not that complicated. When we feel we have to be on the other side of the room, for example, we know we have to be there. We don't wonder why we have to be there, we don't consider what it might be like to be there,

< 13 >

we don't worry about what might happen there, we just know we have to be there, so we go. By the time you've finished thinking about it and decided to go to the other side of the room, we're already there."

I had to think about that for a while before I fully grasped the significance. Obviously this was why my cats, seemingly for no reason at all, would suddenly race frantically through my apartment. The Urge. Or, perhaps more descriptive, the Big Urge. I wondered if that was short for "urgent," because when they raced through the apartment, they seemed to have some urgent task. When I asked Bomber what the Big Urge felt like, he explained, "It's like your life is double-parked and a tow truck has just pulled up. It completely takes you over. It's not just the most important thing, it's the only thing. Most cats will fight their way through any obstacle when struck by the Urge."

"Even Catfish?" I asked. I'd noticed Bomber didn't seem comfortable talking about her.

His whiskers shuddered. "With her it's more of an itch than an urge," he said disdainfully.

It was much later in the evening when I finally gathered the courage to ask the question every person who has ever kept a pet has pondered. "So, how do you feel about me? I've been a good owner, right?" I know what I believed. I believed I'd been a caring, loving guardian, who had ensured the phys-

< 14 >

ical safety of my pets while providing for their crea-
ture comforts—even if sometimes they didn't get
everything they wanted.

Bomber glanced very slowly around the room before answering. It was the familiar cat scan, and I
felt as if he were looking right through me. When he
finally spoke, he carefully avoided answering my
question. "Relationships are difficult," he said halt-
ingly, "particularly between two individuals of different species.

"The most important decision a young kit has
to make," he continued, "is where to live. Where to
shed his fur, if you know what I mean. We have
to be very careful when picking our host—that's
you, by the way; you're my host—because we're going to be living with them for a long time."

I interrupted. "Bomber," I corrected, "you didn't
pick me. I picked you."

"I know," he agreed, without nodding. Appar-
ently cats don't nod. "I know you think that.
Humans always think they're making the big decisions. It's very cute.

"But let me tell you how it really happened. When
we'd outgrown our cardboard box, my mother
managed to get us a cage at the A," he explained, obviously referring to the ASPCA. "I guess I caged
there about two weeks before you came in. I'll never
forget that day. Several people had been there before you, but they just didn't feel right. One of them

came in with a little girl. That eliminated them right away. That's just what I needed, a kid to dress me up in doll clothes. My oldest sister loved being pampered, so she took them. I never saw her again.

"The next couple who came in seemed pretty interesting at first whiff. They smelled of money—literally. He must've worked in a bank or something. I had a real good feeling about them until I heard her mention that they'd just bought a farm in Connecticut. Look at me, David: Is this the body of a mouser? The only way I like my mouse is fillet.

"Then you came in." And as he said that, I thought I noted a slight change in his tone, as if he were savoring a pleasant memory. "Right from the start, I thought you might be all right. You just radiated chicken primavera. I figured you'd had it for dinner the night before. Course, now that I know you better, it might have even been two nights before—no offense. You were wearing a nice sweater, and I could scent the quality of your furniture, so I knew you'd be comfortable. And you didn't have any cat hairs on you. That was important, because it meant I'd have the place to myself. Who knew you were gonna . . ."

His voice trailed off. I knew he was referring to Catfish. "But I got her for you," I said defensively, whispering so she wouldn't hear me. "I wanted you to have company when I wasn't home."

"Thank you very much for asking me how I felt

< 16 >

about it," he replied with just a touch of sarcasm. "Anyway, you came in by yourself. That meant I wouldn't have to break you of too many bad habits. So it was either sit in that cage and gamble that somebody better would come along, or go cute on you. Between staying in a cage and you, you won. Remember? Remember how I started licking your hand?"

How could I forget? He'd captured my heart in a few seconds. He was so small, so vulnerable, so confident . . .

"You'd had blue cheese on your salad, too."

We sat there long into the night recalling those carefree early days we'd spent together, as we'd gotten to know each other. When I told him how proud I'd been when he learned how to use the litter box, for example, he responded by telling me how proud he'd been when I finally learned how to clean it. "Frankly," he added, "you seemed so smart, I was surprised how long it took me to train you. I have to be honest with you, Dave, there are dogs who learn faster than you did, and you know what they say about dogs."

After the failure of my initial attempt to convince Alice that The Bomber could speak and that fiasco at the office, I'd told absolutely no one about our conversations. I'm not a stupid man. I knew what people would think. Instead, I simply canceled most of my plans and went right home after work. I made

< 17 >

up all kinds of wild excuses, and I discovered that people will accept almost any reason for breaking an engagement—except, perhaps, "I have to go home and have a conversation with my cat."

My life with The Bomber had changed completely. For eight years I'd been his guardian, I'd made all the rules, but now we were more like roommates. Each night we'd sit in the living room and eat together. He'd started telling me to bring home specific foods for dinner. He loved beef, chicken, and cheese; he hated Mexican and green vegetables. Often when I'd bring home something new for him to try he'd sniff it and walk away. "How do you know you don't like it without even tasting it?" I'd complain.

"I don't have to," he'd reply. "Haven't you ever heard about the survival of the finickiest?"

Probably the biggest change in our lives concerned our sleeping arrangements. Almost always Bomber had slept on my bed, sometimes under the covers, sometimes right on the pillow next to me. When a woman slept over I often awakened to find that he'd slipped between us. But after he began speaking, the truth is that I felt a little uncomfortable sharing the bed with him. It was no longer as if I were sleeping with a pet; it was more like being with a guy. I slept restlessly for two or three nights, and finally I couldn't take it anymore. We were sleeping back-to-back, and I asked loudly, "Are you asleep?"

< 18 >

He mumbled something.

I rolled over. "We have to talk," I said.

"Tomorrow," he said, nuzzling deeper into his favorite pillow. "I'm tired."

"I really want to say this right now," I insisted.

With an audible sigh he rolled over and barely opened his eyes. "What's the matter now?"

"This," I said. "I'm just not comfortable sleeping with you like this, okay?"

"Can't we discuss this in the morning?" he asked, then closed his eyes and rolled over.

I tried to go back to sleep, but I could feel his overwhelming presence. I lay there for perhaps an hour, listening to the endless din of the ticking clock. It was useless, I realized. I just couldn't sleep with him anymore. There was only one thing for me to do. I shook him awake and told him, "I'm gonna sleep in the living room tonight." I took my pillow, got an old blanket from the top of the closet, and stretched out on the couch. And from that night on, that's the way we slept.

Catfish, meanwhile, was keeping more and more to herself. She refused to join us for dinner in the living room and would eat only when I gave her cat food in her dish on the kitchen floor. Sometimes she'd lie by the heater listening as Bomber and I talked, but more often she'd go into the bedroom to sleep or watch television.

More than a week had passed since I'd seen Alice,

< 19 >

and the tension between us was sharper than The Bomber's claws. I wanted her to share this incredible experience with me, I needed to be able to talk about it with someone I trusted, and I wanted her advice about the best way of proceeding. But I knew that none of this would happen until she spoke to The Bomber herself.

I was very nervous when she arrived. "I know I've been acting really strange," I admitted as I took her coat, "but there's a good reason for that. See . . ." I fumbled for the right words but couldn't find them. I turned to The Bomber, who was splayed on the floor chewing a rubber snake. "You tell her," I said.

The Bomber rolled over with the snake held firmly in his mouth and front paws, and scratched it with his rear claws.

"That's not funny," I told him. "Now come on, say something."

He stretched. I started sweating.

"Don't do this," I warned. "You'll be very sorry."

Alice was trying to remain calm. "What is it you think he's going to do?"

"I don't *think* anything," I snapped at her. "I

< 20 >

know what he's going to do. He's going to tell you that he can talk. Go ahead, Bomber, say something."

Alice laid her hand on my shoulder. "David," she said gently, "cats can't talk."

I shook it off. Large beads of sweat were rolling down my face. I knew exactly what he was doing. "This one can," I insisted through clenched teeth. "He's not talking on purpose. He's just trying to show me up. All right." I surrendered to him. "You win. You can have the pizza . . . with anchovies. All you have to do is ask for it. Out loud." The silence was deafening. "I'm waiting," I said, tapping my foot.

In my mind, I thought I could hear him laughing.

Tears welled in the corners of Alice's eyes. "David," she said in a voice struggling for normalcy, "I know that you really believe your cat can speak to you. But maybe you should think about going back to see Dr. Kleinschmidt. He'd understand this need of yours to . . ."

Bomber purred just loudly enough to catch my attention.

"Wait, wait, wait," I interrupted triumphantly, and perhaps a bit hysterically. This woman, with whom I might possibly have been in love, thought I was crazy, and I was being outfoxed by a cat. "I can prove it, Alice, I can prove it to you." I looked at The Bomber and chuckled. "We'll just see who's the smartest one around here!"

I made Alice sit down and slipped one of the tapes

we'd made into my recorder. It was the conversation we'd had about his resentments, specifically the section focusing on the summer we'd spent in the Hamptons. Bomber complained that he'd worked very hard to catch several voles, small rodents, and had brought them into the house to impress me. Bonding, he'd called it. "And you," he'd said accusingly, "what did you do? You just picked them up and threw them out without even tasting them. How did you know you wouldn't like them without even taking a bite?"

After listening for several moments, Alice looked at me questioningly. "So?"

"So? What do you mean, so? So who do you think that is talking?"

Alice couldn't even look at me. She bit her lower lip. "David," she said in a voice devoid of emotion, "David, if you really want to know, it sounds just like you speaking in that squeaky voice you use sometimes. Your silly kid voice." She covered her mouth with her hand as she searched for the right words. Finally she told me, "I love you, David, you know that. I've always appreciated the fact that you were so different from everybody else. But this . . . I . . . you . . ." She shook her head and her mouth opened and closed, but no words came out. Tears rolled down her cheeks into the corners of her mouth.

I glared at The Bomber. "You just want to make me look like a fool," I said, then warned, "Well, mis-

< 22 >

ter, it isn't going to work. You don't want to speak, fine, don't speak. Don't say one word. But believe you me, you'll pay for this."

The Bomber wagged his tail happily.

"David, stop," Alice demanded, "just stop, please. Please."

The Bomber lifted his leg and began licking his privates. Or at least what was left of them after the operation. I got his message.

Alice practically ran out of the apartment. She refused to listen to any explanations. And, really, how could I explain it? I could lie to her, I could claim I was having a breakdown, or I could defend the truth. But the only thing she wouldn't have believed was the truth. We drifted apart.

For several days after that, The Bomber and I barely spoke. If he didn't want to talk to me, I certainly wasn't going to speak to him. An icy chill descended over the apartment. After all those years of silence, the quiet was maddeningly loud. The few words we addressed to each were spoken with forced politeness: "Excuse me." "Thank you." "Please pass the catnip." I made a point of playing the entire score from the Broadway musical *Cats*, which I knew he hated, over and over. I even tried to punish him by serving him cat food in his old dish. But he simply refused to eat. "It doesn't bother me if you don't eat," I warned snidely, "'cause that's all you're getting, Mr. Cat-got-your-tongue."

"I'm not hungry," he responded. Maybe he took a few bites when I was sleeping, but overall he stopped eating. Catfish didn't seem to mind the turmoil, though; in fact, she seemed happier than she'd been since The Bomber had started speaking. And she even started brushing up against my leg with affection, something she'd rarely done in the past.

After three nights of this cold silence, Bomber couldn't take it anymore. I was reading a Cleveland Amory thriller when he cleared his throat and asked, "You know why the pony wouldn't talk?"

I kept reading. "I don't know, and I don't care," I said.

"Because he was a little horse." When I didn't respond, he continued, "What do you get from unhappy cows?"

"You're not funny, Bomber."

"Sour cream. Go ahead and stop me if you've heard this one: What do you get from Superman's sheep?"

"I'm not listening," I said in a singsong. "I'm not paying any attention to you."

"Steel wool!" After another long silence, during which I pretended to be reading, while, in fact, I'd completely lost my concentration, he finally apologized. "Okay, I'm really sorry."

I put down the book. "Oh? Did I hear somebody say something?"

"I said I'm sorry. Maybe I shouldn't have done that."

< 24 >

"Well, then, why did you?" I asked angrily, "Why'd you have to embarrass me? I mean, what did I do to deserve that kind of treatment? Did I ever make fun of you, did I ever intentionally hurt you?"

In one great fluid motion, he jumped onto the windowsill. He stared into the night as he spoke. The dull glow of the street lamps made him appear to be a more reflective gray than usual. "I'm just not ready to speak to anyone else yet," he said softly. He turned and looked at me. "For more than five thousand years no cat has ever broken the vow of silence. But I thought I could trust you with this knowledge. Believe me, if cats outside this apartment find out I talked, I'll be an outcast for the rest of my lives. And the first thing you want to do is blab it all over the place. Next thing I know you'll have me on *Inside Edition*." A large truck rumbled down the block, rattling the windowpanes. The Bomber waited until it turned the corner, then asked, "If this gets out, you have any idea what'll happen to every other cat?"

Just then, the Big Urge must have attacked Catfish, because she dashed into the living room, circled the couch twice, then raced back into the bedroom, gone as quickly as she had appeared.

"No," I admitted, "I don't."

"Their lives would be a living hell, that's what. I mean, just think about it for a minute. Every cat host in the world will insist that his cat talk to him.

And if the cat refuses—and believe me, a lot of them will; a lot of them still believe in the old traditions— those hosts will be out looking for cats that are willing to talk cute to them. And you know as well as I do, some cats would say anything for a warm house and a few square meals. Old cats will be thrown into the street, or people will try to bribe them by holding back food; they'll stop cleaning their litter boxes, take away their favorite pillows. Absolutely everything we've worked for all these years would be lost overnight.

"Think about it from your side, too. Maybe you've forgotten how easy you had it before I started talking. You fed me whatever *you* felt like buying, changed the litter whenever *you* remembered to, always watched what *you* wanted to on TV, came and went whenever *you* felt like it. You were in complete charge. You had nobody to answer to. Have you noticed how things have changed around here?"

I nodded. He was making a very good point.

"I don't think you realize how lucky you are to have me. We happen to get along very well, but a lot of hosts aren't going to be so lucky. One thing about cats, see—every cat has his own opinion about everything. As we like to mews, one cat's mouse is another cat's rat. Once a cat starts expressing his feelings, forget about it. People are going to be running back and forth to the store all day, cleaning the

< 26 >

litter box four, five times a week, renting the movies the cat wants to see, feeling guilty every time they leave the house. That's not to mention what would happen to phone bills. Believe me, if there were anyone I could call while I was stuck here all day . . . Well, you should be thankful there's nobody else I want to speak to.

"Sure, hosts think it would be so cute if their cats were to speak to them, because they're sure their cats would tell them how wonderful they are and how much they love them. Some of them would, too, but just watch what happens the first time a cat tells his host to take a shower, or accuses him of being too cheap to buy the gourmet cheese. Believe me, cute is not having your cat wake you up in the middle of the night to complain that he's hungry. There's a delicate balance between cats and their hosts. Disrupt that balance and you'll make everyone unhappy." He paused to gnaw at his paw for a moment, then concluded, "You see what happened with us. We got along perfectly for eight years, I start speaking, and a week later we're barely talking to each other." His ears dropped almost horizontal and he said softly, "I don't know if I can speak to anyone else. It just doesn't feel right. Give me a little time."

This wasn't an easy thing for me to accept. I've spent my life as a writer, and the greatest story of my lifetime was unfolding in my apartment. I'd learned

< 27 >

what might very well be the best-kept secret in history, and I was being asked not to reveal it to anyone. I desperately wanted to write about it—desperately. I'd written books with George Burns and Ron Luciano and Leslie Nielsen. Mafia killers had collaborated with me, exposing life inside organized crime. But my cat didn't want me to write a word about him.

This was the career maker, the banner headline, my reservation for a Pulitzer. Obviously I could write about him if I wanted to; he couldn't stop me. But in my entire career, I'd never betrayed a source. So this was a question of ethics. And money, of course. And the fact that the woman I might possibly be in love with thought I'd been playing too long in the litter box of life. I knew it would relieve some of the pressure I was feeling if I could prove to her that I wasn't simply chasing my own tail. If I could share this secret with her, it would be easier to keep it from everybody else. So while The Bomber remained adamant I tell no one, I decided to get proof he could speak, and once I had that proof I'd decide precisely how to use it.

The first thing I intended to do was to convince Alice I wasn't totally insane. After that, I hoped I might be able to persuade The Bomber to collaborate with me on his autobiography. I vowed that under no circumstances would I try to exploit him and decided that at the proper time I'd find

< 28 >

a good agent to advise me how best not to do that.

But proving The Bomber could speak wasn't going to be easy. Tape recordings weren't sufficient evidence. Anybody could be pretending to be The Bomber. I needed real proof.

The Bomber and I got along quite well after our first spat. As he grew to trust me, he began revealing more and more secrets of his world. For me, each night was a new adventure. One night, I came home to find him posing in front of the full-length mirror, his neck stretched as taut as possible. "What do you think?" he asked as he admired himself. "Do I look Egyptian?"

"More Brooklyn," I joked. He was not amused. Like every other cat, Bomber took himself very seriously. His tail brushed unhappily from side to side. "I just wish I could do something about these big ears," he said wistfully.

That night he revealed to me what cats do when left home alone. "Years ago it was so simple," he explained. "We would sleep for a while, then walk around, eat if there was food, then sleep some more. The reason cats like to sleep so much, you know, is because we have such wonderful dreams. In our dreams we're free to play anywhere we want, and we're always safe. Sometimes we dream that we're running through fields of catnip in the spring, or that we're going round and round in an endless circle chasing a mile-long tail. Of course, these dreams are so exhausting that we have to go back to sleep. Then we start dreaming again."

"Do cats dream in black and white or color?" I asked. I'd read somewhere that cats dreamed in shades of gray.

"Virtual reality," he corrected. "Believe me, it's as real as sitting here right now talking to you. We dream in 3-D, Cine- maScope, Smellovision. It's like life, but safer."

"How about games? Don't you play any games when you're alone?"

"Used to," he said. "We used to play all the great cat games. Hide the one sock. See how high you can jump against the white wall. Eat the flowers and see how much you can throw up. That was a great one: I used to love to play hide- the-throw-up-in-a-shoe. Catfish and I used to play knock-stuff-on-the-floor, tear-up-the-paper, break- the-vase, toss-the-roach. Catfish still loves to press the rewind button on your answering machine after someone leaves a message. So there was always something to do."

"What about all those toys I bought for you?

< 30 >

Didn't you ever play with them?" I'd always wondered whether cats really enjoyed playing with those cute two- and three-dollar things I'd picked up at the pet store.

He made big sarcastic loops with his tail. "Oh, whoopee," he said flatly. "Did we love them. Boy, that wind-up mouse was fun to torment. Did it fool me. It looked so real, and I just love the taste of artificial hair in my mouth. And that plastic ball with the bell in it? I could chase that for seconds and seconds without getting bored. And that rubber snake? Oh, I was so scared. I was a regular fraidy cat." He looked at me and said, "Believe me, I'll take a long shoelace or a trapped fly to play with anytime."

"How about . . ."

"But there was one thing I really did like," he interrupted. "I loved that big scratching post. I had the most fun with that."

I smiled. For almost a hundred dollars I'd bought the ultimate in scratching posts, a three-tiered, multi-platform, carpet-covered scratching house. "That makes me happy," I said. "But I never saw you using it. When I'd get home it looked like you hadn't gone near it, and instead you'd been scratching holes in the upholstery. 'Member how upset I used to get?"

"I know," he agreed, "that was the fun part." He mewed again, which I'd begun to understand was sort of a cat chuckle, then asked, "Is there any cheese?"

It was my turn to be amused. Is there any? What he really meant was, would I get up and go into the kitchen and cut him a hunk of cheese? Lately, I'd noticed, he'd become very demanding. He was always polite about it, but he was still demanding. Would I leave a light on at night? Would I turn up the heat when I left for the office? Would I splash some cologne on his litter? Would I give him a clean shirt to sleep on? Small things, none of them too much trouble; but each day it was something else. Slowly he was taking control of my life. As I cut him several slices of cheese in the kitchen, I realized I would have to stop him. "You said that's the way you used to play," I said loudly. "So what happened?"

His voice had limits, I'd learned. For example, he couldn't shout. As I returned to the living room, he replied, "What happened was the greatest single advance for cats since the invention of the mousetrap," he replied.

I put the plate of cheese in front of him. He poked at it with his paw, then sniffed it and finally took a bite. "What advance was that?" I asked.

Bits of cheese fell from his mouth. He looked at me quizzically, as if the answer were obvious. "The television remote control," he said. "That changed everything." He chewed another slice of cheese, then continued: "Hey, there are only so many tails you can chase in your dreams. The difficulty cats had always had with television was that we couldn't turn or pull out the on-and-off knob or change channels. Televisions were basically cat-proof. The remote control changed all that. Even cats without claws can press the buttons."

Suddenly a lot of things made sense. The fact that I could never find the remote control when I came home at night. The fact that when I turned on the TV it was tuned to a different channel than it had been when I'd turned it off. The Bomber had been spending his days watching television. Certainly I'd suspected it. I think every cat host secretly believes his cat spends the day in front of the TV set. But here, finally, was confirmation.

With great curiosity, I asked, "Well, what shows do you like?" It occurred to me that The Bomber's viewing habits might be affecting the Nielsen ratings. Could it be that all across America cats were actually determining the most popular TV programs? On certain levels that made sense: Who else could be watching Regis and Kathie Lee?

< 33 >

Bomber confirmed my suspicions. "My favorite is Vanna. She's so pretty for a woman, and she's such a good speller. And I like Regis and Kathie Lee. That Kathie Lee, she's almost as smart as Vanna. And I like Joan Rivers and *Gourmet Kitchen* and *Gourmet Pasta Chef* and *The French Gourmet* and some of the cartoons. In the afternoon I like *Days of Our Lives* but she" —he frowned; I knew he was referring to Catfish—"she wants to watch *All My Children. All My Litter*, I call it. So we're constantly fighting about it. Then later we watch *Barney, Tom and Jerry, Sesame Street,* and Peter Jennings. Then you come home."

"Peter Jennings, huh?" That was impressive. "So you watch the news?"

"Course. Everything that happens in the world affects cats in some way or other. But I have to tell you, sometimes I really don't understand why humans make such a big deal about things. The whole Bobbitt case, for example. They do exactly the same thing to ten thousand cats every day and nobody says a word, but do it to one man and it's the only thing people want to talk about. I certainly hope chickens don't find out about it, 'cause compared to what they do to chickens . . ." He raised his eye whiskers for emphasis.

"Anyway," he said, finishing the cheese, "that's how the remote control changed the lives of every cat in the country. Now, if we could just figure out

< 34 >

how to work that other thing, everything would be just about perfect."

I thought I knew precisely what he was talking about. "The computer?" I asked.

"Oh, no," he corrected, "the Clapper."

As the weeks rolled by, I got to know The Bomber as I might any close friend. But to my disappointment, Catfish insisted on acting just like a cat—eating from her dish, playing with toy mice, chasing shadows, all of the things Bomber no longer did. She even seemed slightly embarrassed by the privacy screen I'd hung around their litter box. Those things I'd once found so endearing about her, so cute, I now considered silly. She insisted on spending hours slapping with her paw at water dripping from the kitchen faucet, as if the movement and plopping sound meant it was alive. I got irritated when I found her hiding in the clothes hamper. And occasionally now, when Bomber was sleeping, she would go to him and urgently lick his fur, cleaning him, giving him, as Bomber had once described it, "the old soap-and-tongue."

I tried to talk to her about her decision to remain silent. Late one night, as Bomber lay sleeping peacefully in the bedroom, I sat down next to her on the couch and asked softly, "Are you sure there isn't something you'd like to tell me?"

In response, she leaned toward me and licked my nose, then affectionately rubbed her head against

< 35 >

my cheek. But she had absolutely nothing to say.

At times, I admit, I tried to trick her into speaking. While getting ready to feed her dinner, for example, I'd ask in an overly friendly tone, "Cat, you want the sliced beef in thick gravy or the boiled kidney stew?" Of course I knew the answer, but I was hoping she might forget for an instant that she wasn't speaking and respond. Or when I was going to the supermarket, after Bomber had given me his list, I'd ask her, "How 'bout you, Cat? Want me to pick up anything special?"—again, hoping her desire might outweigh her prudence. But she never said a word; she just meowed and purred, often pretending she didn't understand a word I was saying. And I went along with this charade. I had no choice. If she didn't want to speak to me, there was nothing I could do about it.

I stopped trying to convince Alice that The Bomber could speak. We had passed an uneasy few weeks, during which we rarely saw each other. When we did speak, we both danced lightly around the only subject that really mattered. Gradually she softened, telling me that she cared so much about our relationship, she couldn't avoid it any longer. "Are you okay now?" she asked. "I mean, that thing between you and The Bomber. It's over now, right?"

I cleared my throat, then admitted, "Everybody knows cats can't talk." I had to make up a whole story about making up the whole story, and

< 36 >

promised I would never do it again. Only then did she agree to spend the night with me.

I warned Bomber that if he so much as yawned too loudly, I'd never speak to him again. That would leave him imprisoned in our apartment with only Catfish for companionship. He gave me his word as a cat that he would respect my needs.

He also agreed that Alice and I could sleep in the bedroom.

And he kept his word—for most of the evening. But as I was brushing my teeth, he hopped onto the toilet-seat lid. "I'm doing pretty good, right?" he asked.

"Yes," I whispered. "Shhh . . ."

"I haven't said one word all night, right?"

"Just keep your voice down, will you, please?"

He licked his chops. "So, um, what're you doing this weekend?"

I stopped, a strip of blue toothpaste dangling from the tube, and looked at him. "Alice and I are going out to . . ."

Suddenly Alice called from the bedroom, a tremble in her voice. "David, what's going on?"

I narrowed my eyes and glared at The Bomber as I realized what he was doing. Pointing the toothpaste tube at him, I cautioned, "If you think you can . . ."

He started humming. He'd never hummed before. I don't know where he'd learned to do it, and

< 37 >

it was awful. Even for a cat, he couldn't carry a tune. "Cut it out," I hissed through clenched teeth, "right this minute. I swear, Bomber . . ."

There was fear in Alice's voice when she spoke again. "David, please come out."

"All right," I whispered, submitting to his blackmail. "You can come with us."

"Actually, I don't feel like traveling this weekend," he said. "Maybe you should stay in the city."

We just stared at each other for an instant, neither of us blinking. I didn't know what to do. In my anger, I started to raise my hand to hit him; fortunately, I caught myself. Even he wasn't going to turn me into a cat abuser. I could hear Alice stirring in the bedroom. "You win," I spit out. "We'll stay in New York. But keep your mouth shut." He scampered happily out of the bathroom.

Alice was half dressed when I walked into the bedroom. "What are you doing, Al?" I asked wearily.

She continued dressing. "Who were you talking to in there, David?"

"I wasn't talking . . ."

"I heard you," she snapped, as if I'd betrayed her trust. "I heard you talking." She was very beautiful when she was irate, her cheeks the warmest color of blush.

I had to think fast. The one thing I couldn't admit was that I'd been speaking to The Bomber. That would re-ignite the whole thing. Of course, I also couldn't tell her that I wasn't speaking to The Bomber, because then she'd believe I was talking to myself again. Given the situation, there was only a narrow opening, and I ran for daylight: complete denial. "You must be imagining things," I lied seriously, as Bomber came striding purposefully into the bedroom and jumped onto the bed, his tail high and proud. "Who would I be talking to? Him?" I forced a chuckle. "Hey, Bomb, were we talking in the bathroom?"

He didn't say a word.

My relationship with Alice hinged on what happened in the next few seconds. Who would she choose to believe: herself or me? As she made that decision, The Bomber affectionately nudged his head against her leg, demanding her attention. Distracted, she glanced at him and began scratching him. She exhaled, then frowned. "Well, maybe I was just hearing the TV from next door."

"The walls are very thin," I agreed.

In my head, I heard The Bomber reminding me, *You owe me, pal.*

The following night I admitted to him, "You know, you're a pretty clever cat." He might have blushed at the compliment, though it was difficult to tell, with his gray fur.

"You didn't have anything to worry about," he replied. "She wasn't leaving."

"Oh, yeah? What're you, Dear Tabby?"

He rolled over on his back. "Scratch my neck for a minute, please." As I did, he explained, "I know that because I see what goes on here when you're not home."

"What?" I'd heard what he said; it was the meaning that startled me.

He purred, cat shorthand for perfection. "That's nice, right there. Yeah, when you go out and leave her here alone? She's not alone. I'm here, too, and I see what she does. Like sometimes she looks through your appointment book. My guess is she wants to know what you're doing when you're not with her. You know she wouldn't do that unless she really cared about you."

I must have mumbled something in response, but I don't remember. In truth, I was completely stunned. Without realizing it, I'd been living with the perfect security system: a watchcat. A cat who saw everything that took place in my apartment when I wasn't there, every single thing Alice did, and my maid, and the super, and all the repairmen—everything. And no one paid the slightest attention to him. To them, he was simply furniture that moved. "So?" I asked, trying to sound casual. "Is that the only thing she does?"

"Mostly. Once in a while she plays back the messages on your answering machine."

Somehow, the knowledge that she cared enough

to spy made me feel very good. "What else?" I demanded. I wanted to know everything. "What about Ingrid?" I asked. Ingrid was my housekeeper. "What does she do?"

"She cleans, that's all," he said, a bit too defensively, I thought. I wondered if she might be slipping him some extra catnip. That was just like her: trying to bribe him even though she didn't know he could talk. He must've heard me thinking, because he added, "And sometimes she stops to watch the soap operas."

"That's all?" I sensed he was still holding something back.

"Oh, and maybe once in a while she takes a drink from the liquor cabinet," he admitted. "Or two." I stopped scratching. "Or three."

No wonder I'd recently found my underwear washed and dried and neatly folded—in the refrigerator. "Who else?" I asked, scratching again. Who else had been in my apartment and never suspected they were being watched?

The Bomber told me about several other people: the TV repairman who'd taken my high school ring, the former girlfriend who liked to wear my shirts, the super who sneaked in to watch his X-rated movies on my VCR. I listened, fascinated, but I just couldn't stop thinking about Alice. Alice, going through my datebook. Alice, playing back my messages. Oh, how I hoped that some of those mes-

< 41 >

sages had made her jealous. Alice. "Bomb," I asked quite innocently, "have you ever been in love?"

Instantly, a change came over him. Like a clumsy dentist probing with a sharp instrument, I'd struck a nerve. Until this moment he'd had a glib answer for every question I'd asked, nothing seemed to bother him, but suddenly he became silent. He'd been lying on his back, his front legs outstretched as I scratched him, but in response to that question his whole body contracted, and he rolled away from me. "Once," he said finally, "just once. She lived down the block, that apartment with the terrace." Several of the brownstones on West 19th Street had large terraces overlooking the courtyard. Mine was not among them. "She'd stand on the ledge," he continued, and I knew that in his mind he was seeing her again, "and if I squeezed into the corner of the window frame, we could see each other. But there was nothing between us, so we could never get together.

"She was a Persian, what we refer to as an Ali cat. When the breeze was blowing my way I could pick up her scent. She had the glorious perfume of a pristine litter box. She was a natural brown and had long, delicate claws and big, alert ears and the cutest little snout. And her tail . . . She had a long, perfectly shaped tail that seemed to go on forever. And you should have seen the way she could leap and catch bugs in her mouth. She was so graceful . . ." His voice trailed off into the memory.

< 42 >

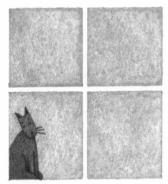

I suppose I heard his feelings more than his words. "Reminds me of Alice," I said.

He must have resented that comparison, because he snapped at me, "Alice couldn't catch a bug in her mouth if she jumped for a year."

I ignored that insult and asked, "But you were never with her. How could you be so sure you loved her?"

He rolled over, twisting his head around first and then letting the rest of his body follow. Now looking at me, he explained, "Love isn't as complicated as humans try to make it. If you have to wonder if you're in love, you're not. It's a lot like the Urge: it's either there or it isn't. For us, it was there. We could just sit there for hours feeling each other's presence. I loved her, I knew it. Believe me, I would've scratched her back."

It was difficult for me to believe that this had been going on right in front of me and I hadn't known a thing about it.

"Sure, we came from different backyards," he continued, "but that didn't matter. We knew we had something special. Every time I saw her my tongue would get all sweaty and my tail would stand

< 43 >

straight up. It was perfect; we never even had the slightest hiss. It went on like that for months, then" —he looked at me sadly—"then fall came, and you started closing the storm windows. We had to stop seeing each other. By the time spring came, she was gone. We never saw each other again."

As I looked at him, I saw a depth of feeling that I'd never before realized existed. I hadn't known he was capable of such deep emotion about anything except food. It seemed so sad, the perfect plot for a French movie. Two lovers separated by an abyss, never to be together. I cleared my throat. "Uh, Bomb, but what about, you know, the physical part of love?" It was such a delicate subject, I was almost too embarrassed to ask about it. "Like, you know, before the operation and all, did you ever have sex?"

His ears perked up at that question. "The birds and the bees, you mean?"

I nodded. "Yeah, right."

His tail started wagging furiously; I wasn't sure what that meant. "That's just typical of you humans. Humans don't know anything at all about that stuff. Pass the potato chips, please."

I did, then asked, "What do you mean?"

"This birds-and-bees stuff. I'm gonna let you in on a big secret. Birds hate bees. They can't stand the little buzzers. Have you ever seen a bird doing it with a bee? Absolutely not. I've never heard one good peep out of a bird about a bee. And trust me, bees aren't so crazy about birds, either. They think they're flighty. So what species do human beings pick to symbolize sex? Birds and bees.

"It's typical, just typical of how confused you people are. You have to make a big deal out of everything you do, just because you do it. Hey, remember, donkeys do it too. So maybe I did, and maybe I didn't. It's not that important. See, animals don't make a big deal out of sex. We don't write books about it, we don't read about it, we don't sing songs about it, we don't watch movies or television shows about it, we don't take photographs or paint pictures of it, we don't buy magazines about it. We don't discuss it, we don't describe it, and we certainly don't analyze it. We just do it. And it feels good. That's it, end of discussion. I don't feel like talking about it anymore."

And he didn't. For the rest of the night he refused to say another word. But this conversation must have upset him, because for the first time in weeks he allowed Catfish to cuddle with him as they slept. He even wrapped his tail possessively over her body. I never mentioned the subject to him again.

As the days became weeks and the weeks eased into months, I never ceased to wonder at this extraordinary circumstance. I never took it for granted. Keeping this secret became so much a part of my life that I rarely slipped, though occasionally in the office I'd accidentally say something like, "Well, as

< 45 >

Bomber was telling me last night . . ." When my friends started talking about their cats, I had to consciously stop myself from correcting their very human misconceptions; and when they bragged that their cats were so intelligent that they knew their names or responded when they heard the refrigerator being opened or had figured out how to open a drawer, I really had to keep myself from telling them that the night before, The Bomber and I had been discussing the meaning of cats in Fellini's movies.

Each night at home was an adventure. The Bomber presented the entire animal world to me, this great gift, night after night. I learned that there existed an entire universe parallel to ours, with unspoken languages and a vast body of myths and folklores and legends. For almost a full winter week, for example, as Bomber and I warmed ourselves in front of a roaring artificial log, he revealed the basis of all cat mythology, the stories that had been handed down for generations from litter to litter, the stories known collectively as "The Cat-o'-Nine-Tales."

"Once there lived in Russia a Great Black Cat," The Bomber had begun. "He was said to be as black as the deepest coal mine, with golden eyes so lustrous that from the reflection of a single candle they could brighten an entire room. He lived in the palace of the Czar, in the very center of Moscow. He

< 46 >

was a very clever cat. In his youth he had been a brave mouser, but as he grew old and whittled he became the mouser supervisor, responsible for the keeping of all the other cats that patrolled the thousand rooms of the palace. It was a great burden, this job, for the palace was very large and the mice had grown bold. But the Great Black did this job well, for he loved his Czar greatly. The Czar was a lonely man who loved precious few things in his life, but among them was the Great Black. They had grown together. The Czar, too, was old, and gone was the passion with which he had once ruled all of mighty Russia. And this was a dangerous thing.

"There was much intrigue within the palace," Bomber continued. In the corner of my eye where illusions live, I saw Catfish steal into the room and settle in a corner as Bomber weaved his tale. "There were many people who wished the Czar replaced by a stronger, fearless man who would attack the ancestral enemies. First among these plotters was the evil Andreas Fydorovitch Kurioski, a name that to this very day strikes fear into the heart of every cat who hears it in his nightmare. Kurioski would not dare strike directly at the Czar, for the consequences of failure were grave and he was not a foolhardy man; instead, he planned to shed the Czar of those few things he held close to his heart. To rob him of all he loved. And when his heart was broken, then Kurioski would move swift and sure, against him.

< 47 >

The death of the Great Black was to be the first of many pains.

"While the Czar was in Kiev, Kurioski summoned the Black to his quarters, claiming that mice had been heard laughing in the walls. It was a ruse, of

< 48 >

course, and the Black knew it, as he knew all that
transpired within the palace, for his cats heard the
echoes of every secret told there. But as an officer of
the Court, he was duty bound to obey his superior.
With a heavy heart he proceeded to Kurioski's
rooms. There he was taken by Kurioski, but as he
was about to be put to death by the sword he spoke:
not as I speak to you, not with words, but with his
eyes and his mind. And with these words that could
not be heard but were spoken just the same, the
Great Black began weaving a wondrous story. Captured by this tale, Kurioski could do nothing save
lower his sword and listen.

"Outside that room, servants also listened as the
dreaded Kurioski became transfixed by the Great
Black, by words they could not hear and so they
doubted were said, and thus began the whispers
that the Black cat was a witch and was to be feared
and had put a spell on Kurioski. Of course, Kurioski
was told none of this.

"On First Night, just before the Great Black
reached the conclusion of his story, as Kurioski reached again for his broadsword, the Black
closed his eyes and seemed to drift into sleep,
though, in truth, while his body rested, his mind remained alert. This catnap lasted through the night,
but as the Black slept, Kurioski could do nothing to
harm him, for then he would never learn the ending
of this tale. And each night, for nine nights, while the

< 49 >

Black sent word to his beloved Czar to return at a mighty pace or all would be lost, he told these stories to Kurioski, always napping as he reached the conclusion. And the nine tales he told are today known to every cat, for these are the stories of who we are."

Just like the Great Black, every night The Bomber would begin one of these stories. But when he neared the end, rather than catnapping to stay alive another day, he'd pause and ask me to pour him a bowl of milk or order a pizza with extra cheese, easy on the pizza. I got him what he wanted as fast as I could, then returned to the fireside. And with this food in front of him, The Bomber would conclude the story of the night.

These were glorious tales—tales of grandeur, tales of deception and betrayal and cleverness, stirring tales of survival, and sad tales. They were the tales that embody the story of a culture. There was the terrifying story "The Monster Who Lived Under the Blanket," which explained why cats have always attacked movement under sheets and blankets. There was the whimsical tale of shrewd bargaining "How the Cat Got His Fur Coat" and the cautionary tale about the dangers of surrendering hard work in favor of luck called "The Cat Who Walked under the Ladder." The courage of cats was celebrated in "The Cat Who Saved Moscow," and their ability to use laughter to escape from precarious situations in "Wearing the Cat's Pajamas." The

< 50 >

reason cats love fish but hate water was explained in the morality tale "The Cat and the Trout," their appreciation of grace and beauty in "The Cat Who Loved Cleopatra," and their ambivalence about humans in "Clawman." Finally, the reason that cats are so independent was revealed in "The Cat Without a Family."

The days passed like a strong wind; I became absorbed in these stories and they dominated every thought I had. And then it was finished. As Bomber told the last of these classic tales, I asked what had a happened to the Great Black. Had the Czar rushed back in time to save him and, by doing so, saved himself?

Rain drumming hard against the windows played a perfect harmony as The Bomber reached the conclusion. "Each morning the evil Kurioski would emerge from his chamber wiping his broadsword and report that the deed had been done, that the Great Black was no more, for he could not risk having the servants doubt his fortitude. Yet the next night, behind securely locked doors, the Great Black would be heard again in Kurioski's rooms. After the ninth night the tale spread throughout Russia of this cat who lived nine lives, and Kurioski became terribly afraid that these superstitious people would rise against him. So there was born the legend that cats lived nine lives.

"The Czar, meanwhile, was rushing back to

< 51 >

Moscow to save his beloved friend. Alas, the winter snows of the mountains blocked his passage. And, in the end, Kurioski killed the cat.

"The Czar indeed fell of a broken heart, but Kurioski was soon lost in the wave that swept over Russia, and then began a time of endless strife in the land that has lasted to this very moment. And that is why forevermore it has been believed that the mysterious black cat brings with him only misfortune."

We sat in silence as The Bomber finally finished telling the stories of "The Cat-o'-Nine-Tales," multicolored flames leaping free of the logs and throwing ragged shadows against the walls, the only sound the dull whir of my tape recorder. He spoke first, asking, "Is there anything else in the house to eat?"

For days afterward I couldn't get this tale out of my mind. Although supposedly working on an article about watching my new car being assembled, in fact I spent most of my time transcribing the tapes. Here was the greatest cat legend ever told, practically the whole story of why cats behave the way they do. From the very first night I thought about publishing these stories as a book, and finally I put aside the car article and wrote as rapidly as possible, trying to catch the flavor of those nights.

I didn't tell Bomber I was doing this, and, truthfully, I don't know why I didn't. The final thing I had to do before sending the manuscript to my agent was type the cover page: the name of the book and the author. *The Cat-o'-Nine-Tales*, I wrote, then stopped. Whose name should go beneath the title? The Bomber's or mine? Should I give him credit for his work? But if I did, people would think I was trying to be cute. No one would believe that he actually told me these stories. Besides, all he did was tell me an old legend. I gave it form. So I typed, "by David Fisher."

Bomber must have heard my thoughts, because a few nights later he informed me, "I'd like to play myself in the miniseries."

In the months since The Bomber had begun speaking to me, my life had changed so radically as to be practically unrecognizable. Once my life had been filled with work and friends, I traveled frequently on assignment, I went out almost every evening. Each day had been different, complete; each day had brimmed with possibilities.

And, of course, with Alice.

My life was simple now: work and home, nothing more. I spent my days writing in my office, most often with the door closed. As much as possible, I avoided assignments that required me to travel for more than a night. My work was suffering, of course, but there was nothing I could do about it. At home I'd rarely answer the phone, and I stopped returning calls that weren't essential. Often I'd let the mail pile up for weeks before opening it; I paid the bills, rejected the invitations, and discarded the rest.

< 53 >

The changes in my life attracted worrisome attention. My friends wanted to help. They asked well-meaning questions: Is everything all right? Is there anything I wanted to talk about? How could I reply: My cat doesn't want anyone to know he can speak?

For a while they tried to drag me out of my privacy, insisting that I join them for the after-work drink or dinner. But I always refused, and eventually they stopped asking, and then they stopped calling. I knew they wondered about the change, but there was nothing for me to do about it. Was I happy? I was beyond happiness; I was obsessed.

And Alice? The distance between us grew wider, yet we were careful not to sever those last threads that held us together. This required a delicate balance—the relationship equivalent of a cat running on fence posts. It meant putting aside the present for the possibility of a future together. But somehow we managed to do it.

My family simply ignored my transformation, loyally accepting every strange thing I did as if it were normal behavior. I sometimes wondered, if I had actually turned into a cat, would they do anything more than compliment me on my choice of coat?

But none of this mattered to me, none of it: not the loss of my old lifestyle or my friends or my lover. My whole life now revolved around those nightly conversations with The Bomber. Obviously, our life together in no way resembled what it had once been. I was no longer his guardian, any more than he was my pet. We lived on almost equal footing now (even though, as he enjoyed reminding me, he had two more feet than I did), with me responding to his needs and desires while he served as my guide through this new world.

Did I still love him? Not as I once had. That cat, that Bomber, was gone. I had loved him selfishly, projecting onto him my thoughts, creating the cat I wanted him to be. In my mind that cat had been helpless without me, vulnerable, and I had been his protector. Now I knew the truth. Did I love him? More than love, I respected him.

Did he love me? That was a difficult subject for me to deal with. It was the one question I just couldn't ask. Perhaps I was afraid of his answer. I think he trusted me, though, as much as it's possible for a cat to trust a human.

Catfish kept more and more to herself. She was always preening, always cleaning, as if she were preparing for some mysterious suitor. On those rare occasions when we did have visitors she would immediately settle into their lap and gaze at them lovingly with her beautiful round eyes. They perceived it as affection; I saw it simply as an obvious attempt for attention. I would have given her that. I would have given her anything she wanted. All she had to

< 55 >

do was ask for it, which she steadfastly refused to do.

Bomber mostly ignored her, which was something I'd never really understood. But one evening, as Bomber was trying to explain cat humor to me, the cause of friction between them was finally

revealed. "I guess the thing that cats think is just about the funniest thing we can do," he was telling me, "is to be real affectionate to people who are allergic to us. It's hysterical, a real tail snapper. See, we know immediately when someone who's allergic to us comes into a room; it's like our fifteenth sense. And there is nothing more fun than jumping

< 56 >

on them and watching them desperately trying to avoid touching us." He mewed at the thought. "The harder they try to avoid us, the greater the challenge. Sometimes it takes a lot of affection, but we get such a tremendous amount of satisfaction watching someone's eyes start to tear, then listening as they begin wheezing and sneezing . . . and that's when we get to ignore them completely."

As I was telling him that I thought that was a pretty cruel joke, Catfish suddenly and inexplicably jumped into my lap and settled there. It had been such a long time since she'd done this sort of thing that I didn't immediately know how to react. She looked up at me with those pleading eyes of hers, then nudged her head hard against my hand, asking me to scratch her head. When I resisted she did it again, this time with more insistence. Finally, I surrendered to those eyes. I began scratching her head. I noticed that she was staring directly at The Bomber, savoring this small victory.

The Bomber stared at me coldly, as if I were betraying him. I looked at him, his front legs stretched out in front of him like the lions guarding the 42nd Street library, and finally broached the subject. "So what is it between you two? I mean, you used to get along so well."

"It's nothing," he said, glancing away as if to deflect the question.

"No, it's something," I persisted. "Come on, tell me."

< 57 >

He stared directly at her for several seconds before admitting, "All right, you want to know, I'll tell you. She's just a dog in cat's fur, okay? Maybe she looks like a cat, but inside that body is the soul of a dog. It happens; nobody knows why."

Although I'd long passed the point at which I could be shocked by his revelations, this truly surprised me. This was blatant prejudice, and I hadn't suspected such a thing existed in the animal world. "Well, Bomb, I mean, what's so awful about being a dog?"

It was his turn to be surprised. His eye whiskers stood straight up. "What's so awful about being a dog?" he repeated incredulously. "Are you kidding me? Have you ever seen a dog?" He almost spit out the word "dog," although his lack of lips prevented him from actually spitting. Still, I'd never seen him act like this before. "Dogs are an embarrassment to their entire species," he began. "The way they'll roll over for a few measly crumbs off the table. Or play dead when a human tells them to. Dead? What kind of game is dead? They lie down and don't move, and people think it's a trick. Believe me, I know dogs; it's no trick. It's what they do best—nothing. And that's supposed to show how smart dogs are? Makes me wonder how smart humans are. You ever see a cat play dead? Absolutely not. And why not? Because cats have integrity and self-respect. We have pride in our genus. Where do you think the word 'pride' comes from? You ever hear anyone

< 58 >

talk about a 'pride of dogs'? I don't believe so."

He was terribly agitated. Obviously, he'd been holding this anger inside for a long time. I couldn't calm him down.

He hopped down from his chair and paced rapidly around the room as he continued. "Dogs actually believe people respect them. Do you believe that? How dumb can they be? It's just ridiculous. They've sold their souls to humans, and for what? I'll tell you. When one human wants to threaten another human with the worst possible thing he can do, what does he say? He says he's going to turn him into dog meat. That's what people really think about dogs. And what do humans call the worst time of the year, when it's too hot to even move and all you can do is lie there? The dog days. Does that show any respect for dogs? No, it does not. But do dogs care? They don't even realize it. They're a disgrace. I mean, you've heard humans saying, 'Lie down with dogs and you get up with fleas.' Is that supposed to be a compliment? Maybe I'm missing something here, but that's what people really think of dogs. They think they're animals.

"But does any of this bother dogs? Not at all. They're oblivious. You notice you've heard of the dog catcher but you've never heard of a cat catcher. You know why? Because dogs have a psychological need to be caught. To be put on a leash and treated like a prisoner. It makes them feel wanted.

"And then if they do get loose, what do they do?

They chase cars. Cars! How incredibly stupid can they be? What would they possibly do with a car if they caught one? Have you ever seen a dog eating a car? No, you have not. Have you ever seen a dog bring a car home? No, you haven't. After all these years, you'd think that by now at least one dog somewhere might have figured out that there is absolutely no reason to chase cars. But no, they insist on doing it, as if they think they're going to catch one and all of a sudden it's going to turn into a huge hamburger." He added in a high-pitched voice, presumably his imitation of a dumb dog, "Oh, no! Metal again."

He was walking in a large circle around the couch. Catfish appeared to be ignoring this tirade, but she stirred in my lap. The Bomber's rant went on:

"Dogs don't understand that people don't respect them. But, I mean, it's so obvious. When a human does something wrong, where do they send him? To the doghouse. But when a man wants pleasure, where does he go? To the cathouse. See? See what I'm trying to explain to you?

"And this scam about dogs being man's best friend? Oh, please. You know why they're man's best friend? Because they never ask to borrow anything, they never make any demands, they never want to discuss their problems, and they never complain. They're happy to eat dog food and live in the

< 60 >

doghouse. Sure, I'd want a dog as my best friend too.

"But no, dogs aren't interested in being *my* best friend. In fact, when they're not busy chasing cars they like to chase cats up trees. And you know why? Because they're bullies, that's why. They have to show their human masters how tough they are by picking on someone smaller than they are, so they take out all their frustrations on us. But even that doesn't work. They never catch us, because dogs are always barking up the wrong tree.

"Just look at her," he said with complete contempt, "look at her lying there." While I thought Catfish looked adorable, he felt quite differently. "All she wants to do is be pampered, be taken care of. Don't you see? She's lost sight of what she is." After a dramatic pause, he pronounced sadly, "She's become a bone eater."

That said, he turned a few tight circles on the carpet, closing in on the precise spot he needed, then flopped down. I didn't know how to respond to his outburst. What terrible thing could have happed to him in his kittenhood, I wondered, to have engendered this hostility? When the feelings in the room had finally quieted, I asked, "Well, Bomb, isn't there anything good you can say about dogs?"

He considered the question for several moments. And finally he decided, "Well, I guess there's one thing. At least they're not chickens. And don't get me started on chickens."

Over the next few days Catfish remained unusually affectionate, insisting on snuggling with me whenever I sat down—and I have to admit I enjoyed it—while The Bomber was aloof. He was in a really cantankerous mood, complaining that everything I did for him was, in his words, "hairball city." And he refused to tell me what was bothering him. During our conversations he was restless and distracted; he couldn't concentrate. I remember one night, for example, when I'd wanted to question him about the unique physical abilities of cats. "How come," I asked, "that no matter how high in the air a cat is thrown, or no matter from what height a cat falls, he always lands on his feet?"

"That's a really dumb question," he replied critically, jumping down from his chair and walking away. "I mean, have you ever stopped to consider the alternatives?"

Nothing could snap him out of his dour mood. I'd completed the first draft of *Cat-o'-Nine-Tales*, and my agent had submitted it to several publishers. The initial response was quite favorable. When she reported this news to me I phoned The Bomber to tell him. This was still before he'd started answering the phone, but I often left him messages by speaking into the answering machine. "You're gonna be a star, Bomb," I said excitedly. That night I brought home a large pizza with three different cheese toppings, but even pizza couldn't cheer him up.

< 62 >

"You sure you don't want to tell me what's bothering you?" I asked.

"There's nothing bothering me," he insisted somewhat listlessly.

"Something's the matter," I said. "You've been really selfish lately."

He objected to that. "It's not selfish," he pointed out. "I'm a cat. 'Member? You scratch my back . . ."

I finished with him in unison, ". . . you scratch my back."

The following morning was so extraordinarily beautiful that I decided to walk to the office. The record-setting snows of winter had melted into weather history, and the first blossoms were proudly showing their colors. It was a perfect New York morning: The air was clear and crisp, the streets were clean, pigeons were clucking, short skirts were back, and I felt a renewed spring in my step. In fact, I wondered if that's why the season was called spring. And then it hit me: spring. It was spring! That's why Catfish had suddenly become so affectionate. And that's what was bothering The Bomber. He had a bad case of spring fever.

On the spot I declared the day a holiday and turned around. The Bomber and Catfish were lounging in the warming rays of the sun on separate windowsills when I burst in. "I've got a great idea, Bomb," I told him. "Let's go for a walk."

He looked at me as if I were out of my mind. "I've

< 63 >

got a much better idea," he replied. "You go for a walk and I stay here. When you get back, you tell me all about it."

I paid absolutely no attention to his protests. I was sure a change of scenery would be good for him. Putting his favorite pillow on the floor of his carrier, I pushed him into it and clasped the wire door shut. "I'm not ready to be outside yet," he claimed.

"And when will you be?" I asked as I put on my jacket.

"When they bring it inside." It occurred to me then that he'd been watching too many sitcoms on television.

For the first time in days he wouldn't shut up. "Whoa now, Dave," he said. "Let's think about this. I mean, do we really *need* to be outside? Don't you know that 'out' is just a quick way of saying 'out of your mind'?"

"Cats don't think," I reminded him, "they feel. Remember?"

"Right," he agreed. "So I feel like I'm going to be sick."

As I carried him downstairs, I saw him jabbing at the door clasp with his paw. "Don't even try," I warned him. "There's no way you can get out of there."

"Get out?" he replied. "I'm just making sure nothing can get in."

I'd actually been very curious about exploring

< 64 >

the world outside with The Bomber. Inside our apartment he was a little lion, a worthy descendant of the king of the jungle, the confident ruler of his domain. But I wanted to see the rest of the world through his eyes. "This is really going to be good for you," I promised, " 'cause I think you've got a bad case of spring fever."

"No, I don't," he responded immediately. "I've had all my shots."

I learned almost instantly how he related to the world outside my apartment: very badly. As we walked along, he wouldn't shut up: "Watch out for that car." "There's a big dog over there. See him? See him? Don't let him get too close." "Don't walk so fast." "Stay away from that Chinese restaurant. I've heard horror stories about their kitchen."

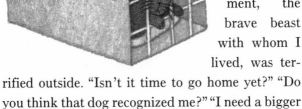

"Don't let that squirrel see me like this." He was unbelievable. The king of our apartment, the brave beast with whom I lived, was terrified outside. "Isn't it time to go home yet?" "Do you think that dog recognized me?" "I need a bigger cage, with stronger bars."

It was difficult to believe that this was the same

< 65 >

cat. He cowered in the rear of his cage, his tail tucked squarely between his legs. He was so scared he didn't care who heard him speaking. Fortunately for him, this was New York City, and anyone who got close enough to hear him naturally assumed I was mumbling to myself and ignored us. When I finally brought him home he immediately ran around the entire apartment, sniffing everything to make sure nothing had changed during the forty minutes we were gone. When he settled down he tried to regain some of his stature. "Well," he said, I suspect mostly for Catfish's benefit, "that was interesting. Let's do it again next spring."

But that brief walk jolted our relationship. I'd been so enraptured with him that I'd willingly allowed him to take control of our lives. The outing had served as an important reminder of just how much he needed me. I think he must've realized that, too, because for the first time he began showing an interest in my life: he started asking me about my feelings. And we never mentioned that day again.

One night it occurred to me that while he spoke reasonably good English, I was completely illiterate in his language. So at my request he started teaching me the language of Tail. It was theoretical, of course, as I lacked the basic equipment. But I was fascinated to learn that Tail is one of the most ancient of all languages, that hieroglyphics showing

< 66 >

cats using a language remarkably similar to modern Tail had been found on cave walls in Mesopotamia. Even more significant, as he proudly reminded me, while there is still no universal language enabling people from different parts of the world to communicate without an interpreter, for thousands of years cats of every breed from all parts of the globe had been able to understand each other without difficulty. Although, he added, certain European cats, notably Italians, also tended to speak with their ears.

"Probably the most significant different between English and Tail," he explained patiently, "is that while English is used to express thoughts and ideas, Tail is used to convey feelings. In fact, Tail is often called 'the language of feelings.' Supposedly, tens of thousands of years ago, humans had tails. But even then humans wanted to hide their feelings, so clothes were invented primarily to cover their tails. And gradually, those tails disappeared."

To my great surprise, he explained that elements of Tail had actually become part of the English language. "English is a scavenger language," he said. "It's primarily a collection of words and punctuation adapted from older languages, and one of those languages is Tail.

"In English, for example," he continued, sounding very much like a small, furry professor, "to indicate excitement or emphasize a strong feeling,

< 67 >

an exclamation point is used. Where do you think the exclamation point comes from? It's well known that this punctuation mark is simply a visual representation of a rigid tail, which means precisely the same thing! The question mark is nothing more than an illustration of a curved tail, showing apprehension or a lack of clear understanding. And other punctuation marks—the comma, the dash, the parenthesis—are adapted directly from Tail."

This was utterly fascinating. Although I knew that, lacking a tail, I could never become fluent, at least I could understand it. That would give me the kind of access to the cat world that no one before me had ever enjoyed. Knowing that my tape recorder couldn't possibly capture the visual beauty of this language, I took notes as he continued this lecture. It occurred to me that Bomber and I might collaborate on a

< 68 >

textbook, *Understanding Basic Tail.* I could even teach it at the New School. But first I had to become proficient in it myself.

"Tail isn't very difficult to learn," he said, "although it does have a lot of subtleties. When you study most languages you begin by learning the basic parts of speech. We begin with the basic parts of the tail. For communication purposes, the tail is divided into three parts, which may be used in any combination. These consist of the whole tail, the half tail, and the tip, or swash. The whole tail is used to convey an overall response, while the half tail and the tip are used for emphasis or clarity. For example, when we get something we really want without too much difficulty, we'll respond with a rigid tail, showing pleasure. Or, as humans might say, we got it whole tail.

"The tip is used to convey feelings of much less intensity. These feelings are known as demi-tails, or de-tails. So while the whole tail expresses the overall feeling, the tip provides the details.

"In addition to the three parts there are also three basic positions: up, out, and down, which is also called the hang or the droop. The meaning of these positions is pretty obvious; food is up, the vet is down. And then there are the basic movements, the building blocks of Tail. These include the familiar wag, the flip, the slap . . ." I was writing furiously. "Don't worry," he said, "I'll go over all of this again

< 69 >

later. So there's the slap, the tuck, the curl, the ring, the nine, the triple lutz, the flopover, or wraparound, and the spiral. And, as with every language, there are some cats who are extremely erudite and have mastered its intricacies. I've heard that some Siamese actually speak in knots, including the legendary figure eight.

"Direction can be very important, too. The direction of the curve of the tail is used to show possession. If my tail is curved inward, for example, toward my body, that's possessive, meaning 'I want' or 'I need' or 'give me.' But if my tail is curved outward, away from my body, that expresses the much more general or inclusive case, meaning 'I want *you* to give me.'

"In a lot of these movements Tail is remarkably similar to Snake, although Snake is a much more rudimentary language. For example, a rigid tail can have several different meanings, but a rigid snake can mean only that the snake is dead."

I felt as if I were back in second grade listening as my teacher, the ironically named Mrs. Katz, tried to bang the English language into my thick skull. But The Bomber was very patient with me. "With practice," he said supportively, "anybody can get the hang of it. Of course, it's a lot easier if you have a tail. But the real beauty of this language comes when all the elements are combined into the flow. Putting these elements into flow is like putting

< 70 >

words into sentences. I mean, whole stories can be told in flow. No one knows the derivation of flow, but obviously it's an imitation of a natural movement. There are some cats who believe it can be traced to the swaying of the reeds blowing in the breezes along the ancient Nile, but its influence can be found in everything from Tail to the hula dances performed by Polynesians.

"There are other things to be considered, too: slim tail or fat tail, and tail speed. Tail speed is a little like punctuation. There's fast, slow, and stopped. By combining all of these elements of formal Tail, we can convey any feeling we want to express. A fast-moving rigid tail, for instance, indicates happiness, while a slow curl of the tip shows apprehension. A full tuck is fear, while the flopover, or wraparound, in which we lay the tail over an object, indicates ownership or affection."

I glanced at Catfish, who was sleeping soundly in a ball, her tail tightly hugging her body. "What's that?" I asked.

"Inside tuck," he replied. "I guess she's feeling a little insecure."

"Ha!" I said. "Can you blame her?"

I noted just a brief slow wag of his tip, but then he caught himself. "You can show almost any feeling you want with a properly expressive tail," he continued: "curiosity, embarrassment, interest or boredom, anger, enthusiasm, attraction, frustration, fear, you name it. Love, hunger, delight or disappointment, loneliness, confusion, sorrow, anticipation, or any degrees of any of them. An almost whole tail with just a little twist of the tip, for instance, means something is very good, but not quite perfect. That might be my way of showing how I feel about a big dish of cream cheese with cashew nuts in it."

Our Tail lessons went on for almost a week. Tail is an amazingly expressive language for those who truly understand it. There was one thing he didn't cover, though, one thing about which I'd always been curious. "Bomb," I asked casually, "why do you chase your own tail?"

He answered immediately, "Because it's there."

Later that night, without my even having asked it, he answered one other question, the question he'd avoided answering so many months earlier: How did he really feel about me? I was sprawled on the couch watching a movie when he lay down right next to me, then nonchalantly laid his tail over my leg. It was just a simple flopover, but it spoke volumes. Words can't express how good that made me feel.

An odd thing happened over the next few days. As I looked at people on the street or in my office, I imagined that they had tails and that by looking at them I could tell exactly what they were feeling. It gave me a tremendous advantage. No wonder people didn't want tails. As I walked down Madison Avenue, for example, I saw an attractive, very well

< 72 >

dressed woman with her tail wrapped around her waist, what The Bomber would have described as "tight-tailed," meaning she was very defensive. For months I'd wondered if the homeless man begging for loose change on West 51st Street was actually as desperate as he appeared to be or was simply playing on my emotions, but when I saw his tail hanging so sadly there could be no doubt. I put a buck in his hand, causing his tip to wag slowly. As I approached the office I passed a group of young children on a class trip, their tails wagging excitedly at top speed. Later that day I was sitting in my office when a very pretty editorial assistant delivered an edited manuscript, and as we spoke I noticed the tip of her tail circling warily with interest. Seeing that, I suggested we have lunch one afternoon, and her tail immediately straightened in response. That same afternoon I smiled quite contentedly when a pompous business writer came out of the managing editor's office with his tail between his legs. I didn't need to consult my notes to understand what that meant.

Even though I knew these were just my fantasies, it was clear to me that life would be a lot less complicated if people still had tails. Certainly relationships would be easier. I also noticed something about myself: Whenever I thought about Alice, I couldn't keep my own tail still.

Almost a year had passed since that fateful evening The Bomber had first spoken to me.

< 73 >

I'd given up completely trying to convince him to speak to other people, as well as secretly gathering proof that he could talk. That would have been a betrayal of our friendship—something I absolutely refused to do. I also gave up all attempts to get Catfish to speak. I accepted her decision to pretend she couldn't.

So the fact is that I wasn't at all prepared for what happened. It began one evening in mid-June as The Bomber and I were watching a Yankee game. I was trying to teach him a little about baseball; naturally, he was a big Tiger fan. During the game my brother, Richard, had called to invite me to his home for the family Father's Day celebration. A few minutes after I'd hung up, I noticed that The Bomber's tail was in a complete droop, his ears were flat, and he looked about as sad as I'd ever seen him. "What's the matter with you?" I asked.

Without lifting his head, he replied, "I'm missing something."

I took a deep breath. This was a discussion I'd been anticipating for a long time. It had occurred to me that on some deep psychological level he'd never really forgiven me for forcing him to have that operation. I'd been waiting for him to bring it up, trying to find some way of apologizing. "You're right," I agreed, "and believe me, if there was anything I could do to replace it, I mean, anything at all . . ." I shrugged helplessly.

He lifted his head. "That's not what I'm talking

< 74 >

about. I'm talking about my family. My mother, my litter. I don't know what's happened to any of them. For all I know they could be living in an alley somewhere, without even a bowl of their own."

My heart just broke for him. "Bomb . . ." I began.

"Sure," he interrupted, "you've got your family. You've got your parents and your brother and his wife and kids, and your sister. You've even got nieces and nephews. Who do I have? I barely remember what my mother smelled like."

I tried to think of words of solace. "Well, you know, I mean, maybe you're lucky. Nobody gets to pick their relatives. Look at it this way: every family has its black sheep, and . . ." I caught myself, then explained, "Of course, that's just a saying. Cat families wouldn't actually . . ."

"Thanks for trying to cheer me up," he said sadly. "But the truth is that on holidays, even if I wanted to go out, I have no place to go."

I began gently stroking the back of his head, and as I did the right words came to me. "I know it's rough, but you've got a family. You've got a family right here that loves you very much. You and me and Catfish, we're a family. Oh, sure, maybe we're not your typical American family, but we live together with trust and we rely on each other for love and compassion and understanding. I know that if I ever need a friendly paw you're gonna be right there for me, and I think you know that whenever you need a chest to lie on, my chest is yours. You know

< 75 >

that no matter what happens in life, through the good times and the bad times, I'll be right there to help you. That's what a real family is. That's what we are to each other."

I could see I had hold of his attention.

"That's right," I continued, my voice growing stronger. "We picked each other. We weren't forced together by fate. I saw you and I wanted you; you smelled me and you wanted me. And we know more about each other right now than most people who were born into the same family. So if that's not family . . ."

"Thanks," he said. "Thanks."

We sat there in silence as I lovingly petted him.

He must have really thought about that because several days later, to my incredible surprise, he suggested, "Why don't you invite Alice over one night?" Then he added meaningfully, "There's a few things I'd like to tell her."

I stammered, trying to hide a smile. "You mean you'd speak to her?"

"Oh, don't make such a big deal out of it," he warned me. "By the time I get through you'll be wishing I'd never said a word. I'll bet you she'd like to know who was making all those hang-up calls."

Alice and I had spoken only infrequently during the past few months. I had no idea how she felt about it, if she even thought about me anymore. Maybe she was seeing someone else. The one thing I

< 76 >

knew for certain was that I missed her very much.

When I called she was reluctant to see me. "I don't want to start that all over again," she explained patiently. "It's just too painful."

"Things are really going to be different this time," I promised. "You'll see."

She was very suspicious. "Why? What's changed?"

"Everything," I told her, "absolutely everything."

For a week before my date with Alice I gave The Bomber every opportunity to change his mind. "Just tell me now if you're not going to talk to her," I pleaded. "That's all I'm asking from you."

"She's really gonna be surprised when I say hello, isn't she?" he asked. I could see he was looking forward to this, too.

Two nights before my date, The Bomber sneezed. It wasn't a big sneeze, but he wasn't a big cat. Within a day the cold had overwhelmed him. He was exhausted, listless; he could barely move. I was so concerned, I wanted to take him to the vet, but he insisted through his stuffed nose, "I'mb hokay."

The lights in my apartment were dimly lit and soft music was playing when Alice arrived. She looked even more beautiful than I had remembered, and the moment I opened the door I knew two things with absolute certainty: I loved her, and I would never let her go again. I realized then that as much as I loved The Bomber and Catfish, they

< 77 >

would have to accept the fact that I needed Alice in my life. Maybe, I hoped, we could all be a family.

I wondered how she felt. If only she really had a tail, I thought.

As she walked in she rubbed Catfish on her head, then noticed Bomber lying in a heap next to the heater. "Hi, Bomb," she said.

This was it. This was the moment I'd been anticipating for more than a year. I looked at Alice, then glanced quickly at The Bomber. I waited, my whole body tensed. Finally, finally, he opened his mouth to respond—and not a sound came out. Not a peep, not a wheeze—nothing. Bomber had laryngitis. He kept trying to speak, and eventually managed a slight wheeze.

Alice became very concerned. "Is he all right?" she asked.

"He's got a bad cold," I admitted.

"Whissssizzzzz," Bomber said.

We stayed there just long enough to have one glass of wine. I felt so comfortable with her, so warm. It was as if we'd never been apart. As we got ready to leave for dinner she stopped at the front door, put her hands on my shoulders, looked deep into my eyes, and said, "David, I just want to tell you how happy I am that you've given up pretending that The Bomber can talk to you."

I glanced at him over her shoulder. He was looking right back at me. Perhaps he was smiling. I hoped so. "Listen," I told her, "I don't give two wags if he never says another word."

And then we left. But just as I closed the door behind us, I heard for the first time the sweetest little voice, and she said, "Oh, he's just a big jerk anyway."

< 79 >